Poems

from

the Website,

“Poetry in Baltimore”

Books by David Eberhardt

The Tree Calendar
blue running lights

DAVID EBERHARDT

Poems

from

the Website,

“Poetry in Baltimore”

LOCH RAVEN PRESS SYKESVILLE, MD 2011

One great thing about print on demand? You can change stuff—just as Shelley or Keats would have liked to. Here are some of my candidates for titles which I cannot choose between—I am open to other suggestions—I'll pay 50 bux to anyone who can give me a title that will last.

Remember, it has to go w painting "Evening Rain" by Ian Sheldon—so?: "Epiphany?, Et Lux Perpetuam, The Celesta in Bartok, Korngold, Shreker, and Strauss, Rampant Lizards, Cellophane Seas, This is Earth, 'Trees like to rot in the forest', my pa liked cheese and crackers, the Constellation EEYORE, An Ecology of the Virunga Range, We all have our secret thoughts, Dunes and Shoals of Alberta?"

After years of searching (approximately 2003 – 2010) for a community of poets, PIB finally gave me what I was looking for, all of us commenting on each other's work and chatting—I had always envisioned and longed for it but never found—now here it was in cyberspace—thanks to Julie Fisher, site mother superior and dominatrix.

Also, thanks to Jim Doss, editor of the Loch Raven Review, Dan Cuddy, Chris George, Keith Hamilton, Constantine Pantazonis and Cathy Permut and all companion poets on PIB.

~ D.E.

Printed in the United States of America

Cover Art: "Evening Rain" by Alberta artist, Ian Sheldon
Cover and book design: Jim Doss

Library of Congress Control Number: 2011943397
ISBN 978-0-9821854-2-1

Loch Raven Press
140 Milrey Drive, Suite L
Sykesville, MD 21784
www.lochravenpress.com

Table of Contents

Poems

from

the Website,

“Poetry in Baltimore”

"Trees like to rot in the forest"

– the Tinklers, legendary Baltimore singing group

(how past loves inform present ones. . . approaching death what becomes important. . . how we affect others, lovers, what they take from us. . . the levels of sentience in all living things. . . wanting to possess the most valuable thing as we are taken away to dust and silence. . . rehearsing death, rehearsing)

At last I know how a tree feels

Aware of all my levels at night,

The dignity of earth in Spring—

Moonlight on the floor, awake at three.

Awake at three I can inhabit

The sleeping earth and think deep thoughts:

I could have loved you so and did!

I know my love made a difference!

Now you are dead—the moonlight shakes

Like Cocteau said—"You do not dedicate

Yourself to poetry, you sacrifice to it".

What did he mean? Who gives a shit!

I try to think now that you're gone

(And you meant the world to me and others!)

Because the night brings on its dreams:

What incubus or meaning in its black seams?

My fingers get numb more now, but as they dry
I can plumb deeper in another sense:
The moonlight of past loves slips by
Your passing has killed two already, but I?

I understand it—I do not need to know.
Where the dead go. Because it's Spring
The trees are in touch with their extremities, they know
What sleep means, just as we know.

The levels of love moving as I love now?
That's probably most important—how...
How present loved ones tomorrow morning wake?
I pray the Lord my soul to take?

In the Constellation Eeyore

In memory of fellow Baltimore poet, David Franks, read at his memorial

Who are you, who do you think we are?

It's all so far, so far, so far.
Start in the constellation "Eeyore"—that guide star. . . .
Pin a tail on it—go from there south in the southern sky. . .

That shadow had not looked that way before,
And since I'm asking why:
Vast forests to the north, bor-

eal taiga, the last time I saw my father,
Spoke to him—I can't remember now.
There could be meaning, could be some how

Like the overtones to a piano string,
The clouds keep changing now that you mention it.
My pa liked cheese and crackers, that I know.

The forests of the night sky, forests of stars
Where you can go a long way before you meet another.
It's all so far, so far, so far.

Who are you, who do you think we are?

Dave reads at memorial for David Franks, Baltimore poet. Dave Eberhardt is sponsored by ju ju froots and pampers

Great Apes

O this world of sad disappearances—another species gone today, I felt it

Slipping—I don't think I can do without the great apes!—militias filtering through

The forests—paws sold for rifles, mountains silver moonlit—silver back

Paws made into ash trays—"Abner" gone last year, "Flora" bereft of her children—

"Soo", "Silver Junior", one night nest left empty forever—Ruwenzori Mountains,

The Virunga Range, Ruwanda, Ruwenzori, H. R. Haggard—Solomon's Mines undiscovered!

I loved how they'd charge up and then just grumble—stomachs rumbling

The nonviolent ape families, for centuries bothered by no one and secure!

Last night I woke and you weren't there either—maybe down the hall reading

In the "commons"—I'm always dreaming of college, dreaming of mom dead last year. . . .

Males play fighting—dangling on "tse nom ba ba" tree branches. . . .

Dreaming of silver dorms how they bleed into mist and into lost begonia forests,

Giant begonias and nettles peculiar to ecosystem. . . rain seeping down always. . . .

Tanzania, Virunga, Ruwenzori, I go looking for you and the treasure but it's gone!!

Along with you, in my dreams looking for Dian Fossey now—murmuring "Fossey". . . "Tanzania"*. . . .

* *emphasize every syllable for the music of it*

A Report from the Front

To Charlie Stine, Maryland environmentalist

The skinks, the newts, the Allegheny hellbender whose range
Has shrunk up next to nothing, Chesapeake Bay
That I would put up there beside Maine/California coast—although a gentler beauty—
The shore not of rock, but rather oaks and holly...

Has also been diminished thanks to new pirates—
Same species as John Smith who saw
We lived with bounty, us—homos, not "sapien" but
Homos Unknowing—new pirate: "developers",

Overfishers—it's us!—just like
The tribes who warred before us—Susquehannocks, Cecil Calvert...
Squabbling about Kent Island—all this history
You were never taught—and so much more to uncover...

You think ELF wrong to blow up radio towers, was anyone hurt?
Let's stand up for the species that were lost today!
Earth Liberation Front!—that's it: spring peepers, tree frogs send
Their message in unison—You humans mark "THE END!"

Maryland cypress swamp

To Ida

(pronounced Ee-dah when spelled out that way—otherwise—I-(eye)-dah (for variety)) This 47 million year old fossil was discovered in Germany.

Bless all star voyagers from the Messel Pit:
The small Creodont, early Pangolin,
Marsupials, lemur like prosimians,
Elegant early hedgehogs, jewel beetles,
The Messel bird, enigmatic owl/hawk combo!
The Massillaropter, tiny hoopoes, hopping horses....

Bless these fossils, but bless especially
Ee-dah—Darwinius Masillae, my Ida!
Who stood at a fork in the road pointing HUMAN!
Bless Ee-dah who for 47 million years
Until pulled from the quarry on a shale slab,
Slept dreaming—bless all travellers! I dream

Of a blue city in the distance—my home—
Purposeful, realized, I can see it
Far way in blue haze, Oz-like from this rest stop
On the thruway in the mountains—I can't get there!
No access to on ramp—stuck in the parking lot....
Like Ida on her bier, resin around me like amber.

O strange sad condition—endless travel, suddenly stopping,
Never getting anywhere! Ee-dah were you heading
Towards the apes—humans or the lemurs?
O Ida, Ee-dah where are we going? in what direction?
The asphalt of parking lots a calm, dark blue,
The blue city on the plains mirage blue.

Orion

*Homage to images in movie "**10,000 BC**"*

I left the village, said good bye to the elders.
The white spear came with us—we entered the "dream time".
Men on horses took her—the one who had pointed
The star light to me—"See that one? Others move but it doesn't…"
And so she remains in my heart, whom I called "Mireille"*.
"We are one—I will "wolf you"**, she said.
Those who took her, tho'—they had worse enemies
Than us—the Ore-Ded***—the ones without seers—
With no one to study star motion.
But we follow Orion—Rigel, Bellatrix, Mitaka****
Canis Major leading ahead like a pointer—
The "white spear" in the heavens and
I take solace in stars and star motion, I will find her!!

* *in the Arcan language—"M'l'r'y"*
** *in the Arcan language—meaning "we will make love"*
*** *Arcan for "military-industrial complex"*
**** *all stars in the constellation Orion*

21st Century Man, a Portrait

He stands outside the Dr.'s office—his only useful function—
A coat/towel rack—because a four hour erection
Has left him permanently stiff—
The side effect of sex enhancing drugs—

After the vasectomy, he'd contemplated matching tubs—
A lady friend—a sunset that's sublime—
And now he stands there; even health care reform
Can't cheer him, the drug has also left him blind!

Labor Day

To long haul 18 wheelers—teamsters, unions, assembly lines,

The friend of labor is a friend of mine!

At hearings, Bobby K tars H w communism—he snaps back: "Never—
No".

J's violence all American—firebombing to show—

Management's supposed power will cave

From Detroit Wheel to Dayton Tire—the worker's not a slave!

Jimmy abducted from Machus Red Fox, 15 Mile at Telegraph, the
spot's

Now Andiamo's, an Italian chain, and it's not

Hard to figure out what happened: Union politics or personal vendetta—
Jimmy's gotta go!

The likes of Tony Giacolone, Tony Pro. . .

Just google FBI report run by once great Detroit News—

American labor 2012 seems in a snooze.

The left built labor—Management will cave!

To organize, to strike—they're not forgotten words.

Yr. 8 hr. day, 40 hr. week, yr. overtime?

Yr. friend of labor is a friend of mine.

Note: I met Hoffa and Provenzano at Lewisburg Prison—Hoffa told a protester/friend: "You guys aren't getting anywhere (w non-violent protest)—You need fists and guns!"

Report from the Front Lines: Iowa State Penitentiary

Inmate A to 4 point control—where are his g d meds?!?
Station 4, Christ stumbles, falls to the road.

Inmate B, gay in Iowa, very young—"red light over my head";
Can we wash Jesus' hair after he's dead?

Inmate C looks "most female, call me 'Countess'", but the guard
Says, "Disciplinary detention"—Jesus' dying is hard.

Inmate D, 2 lifes and change—"dad chokin on mom…
My little brother and I"… he can't remain calm…

Christ borne down from the cross and his beautiful hair
Is all matted, but Mary his mother is there.

Inmate A can go back to his seg cell, we assume
No longer a danger—and so Christ to the tomb.

Prison Poem

Whitney's on the Oprah show again…
"Are you still doin drugs?"…pause…sigh…immm…"Oh"…

And Maury's bleepin out—the whole bleepin show!
And now Whitney's found some religion and then…

"Bleep you", no, "bleep you—you're NOT the father"….
Whitney'd "lost touch with her soul" but she'd rather

Honor her abusive husband than leave…"nowhere to go,
And then moms came and rescued me"…so,

Oprah sits a ga ga—"I'm connecting
With you spiritually", and Maury? He's conjecturing…

"You had an affair and that baby's not yours…
The lie detector test says so," the girl friend bleeps a curse!

Was that a car alarm I heard outside beeping?
No it's just the Maury show in the "common room" a bleeping.

Into the common room, the inmates come and go,
Speaking of Whitney and the Maury Povich Show.

Two Serial Killer Portraits

1. Jeffery Dahmer

His father insisted that he open that one box—

(With head/genitals inside)—his method of mastery—of complete control.

"I suppose we all have our secret thoughts."

A guard sits near as Jeffrey Dahmer talks—

To Stone Phillips of MSNBC—mask of normality over all—

As the serial killer reveals much—unlocking shocking locks:

How he was almost caught—the dessicated rock—

Hard corpse part in its barrel, (dismemberment played a role—)

He needed to keep these zombies near, he needed that control.

I think of Nixon, Bush—their "acceptable dishonesty" as they kill,

And how we all compartmentalize and put away the secrets...

O so heavy—know there will be reckoning, long to be caught!

America's serial monsters—some blatant, others not,

The things unsaid—of sex, of death—of controlling, icy mothers. ghoul-

ish fantasies as lust builds, makes a mock

Of reason; that first hitchhiker, once drugged, the first soldier in Iraq,

And Bush would have to kill again—the "frozen seas within"* he's more and more cold....

The control we need, perfection, the monstrous avatar grows old.

"I suppose," Jeff says, "we all have our secret thoughts."

* *Kafka—"We must take an axe to the frozen seas within us."*

2. Theodore Bundy

after the movie

"Bundy—an American icon"—original title for the mo-
vie, "Daylight exteriors always shoot the fastest; you
Really see the blood, witness the death rattled expiration"!

"The mass of men live lives of quiet desperation"*;
Ted Bundy becomes a Christian at the end;
The dangers of pornography the explanation he offers you.

But lust is good—it's violent lust that's bad—American males a study in
Immaturity, impotence, warfare, gunplay, jealousy, finally—no education;
Woman but an object, mere light between the graveyard yews;

Ted Bundy returns to his corpse—he dresses her anew;
Fucks her dead ass, howls over her like a wolf!
Bites her, she will not fool with him again!!

The Bundies and the BTK's** all had their explanations—
Their origins, their sad childhoods gone askew....
But, hey, this would not be like me and you!?!

"Necrophilia", "ligature", "strangler", or, "sexual asphyxiation",
Holden Caulfield wisely found all adults phony, bogus, nor would you
Find in US literature much authentic emotion—etc.

* *Henry Thoreau*
** *Bind, Torture, Kill*

Homage to Horror Movie: "The Ring"

After my dreams, I'm grateful for the light of day.
It gives solutions to problems of the night.
I hope death will not be an end, just some sort of night.

A burning tree.... I guess I understand. I pray
The demon girl will not come out of my tv today.
The *ladder* then—this also seems to do with night.

Why? Why? would they hurt a child in this way?!?
And why a *light house* with its "tell" and "tell" tolls,
As if singing, like an evil *bell....*

The *horse* pushed off a boat?
My dreams are seldom happy, they're in a sour way—
"You'll have to die", but I wake every day!!!!

I'm happy to be alive—take just last night:
I dreamt of descent, down, down a *well*,
But by the day I'd clambered towards the light—
A glorious spider creature, I woke to bright light!

Thoughts for Those Left Behind

In Memoriam—L. E.

The Ketef Hinnom silver amulet,
Probably a charm,
From 4 to 500 BC...
Unrolled, it still shines!
A first—first discovered
Written down words from the Bible...
Way back in the burial
Chamber, back under more recent stuff
Broken, looted—some sort of scroll:
But still, once unrolled, the old benediction
Across all the years
Keeps coming and coming:
"May the Lord bless and keep you,"
Beside the ticking IV.
"May the Lord cause his/her face to shine upon you"
Since it's so shiny.
Scroll rolled up—cigarette size...
"Grant you peace/comfort."
Scroll finally unrolled.
The horror of operations,
ICU's, visiting rooms...
"And give you peace."
(read in Aramaic first if possible)
"May the Lord bless you and keep you.
May the Lord cause her/his face to shine upon you.
May the Lord lift up his/her countenance upon you!
And give you peace!!"

A few days later a second, angrier poem came to me:

2.

Everyone's death is perfect—the way
Death whisked you away. It took my breath away!
You didn't have to suffer/linger—undergo chemo, long days
Knowing end is coming, heavy goodbyes said all ways...
I know it surprised you as you gulped for air to stay
Alive—you did not have the time to say:
"This is a good thing" (like when ice booms and cracks, fills up the bay?)
At Turkey Cove, bottom of winter, nothing gets in the way
Of cold advancing—buoys unbobbing, even fog horn has no say...
Because—no fog—although the Point Light beams its reassuring way...but
It will not beam for you, "blessedly", not one more day.
If you'd had the time to say it, you'd say:
"I love you, life good/life fast—now...Go away!
Go away long days of suffering...out! Out!! Away!!!"
No coming back, not longing to stay...

Haiku: Notes for a "Villanelle"

1.

Mom dead. . .
i feel the heat
leaving her body.

2.

like an eclipse—
that steady,
only faster. . . .

3.

her body
on a gurney—-
rag heading towards cinders.

4.

her "soul flying
over loch raven"—
people murmuring bull shit.

5.

Vermeer's "Lacemaker"
absorbed, silently
attentive. . . .

“Villanelle” from the Haiku

Mysterious paintings by Vermeer?... the quiet in
Them—woman weighing pearls, sunlight on her face...
My mom’s death got me thinking—drew me in

To Vermeer-thoughts: how “within”
His women seem—one pregnant, His wife?, his “Lace-
maker”—silently absorbed, attentive, sinking in...

When mom died I could feel heat leaving
Her hand as I held it—a surprise, the steady pace—
Like an eclipse, much faster, then her body carted off on

A tray—mere rag headed to cin-
der, but then—consolat-
ion—calm as if in Vermeer’s paintings—it sinks in!

The bull shit comments from those around
Trying to be helpful: “her soul flies out over the lake”, yes—but the bas-
ic mystery-sadness—horror—draws me in.

The blues these women painted in, and pin points of white
That Vermeer uses giving photographic feeling, a slight
Of hand—brush strokes blur into real light.

I write to make sense of it... in the end:
The mystery of mom’s death draws me in!
The silence—Vermeer paintings... it sinks in!!

Three Anti-War Pieces

1. in memoriam: originally read in honor of my dear friend and accomplice—Tom Lewis—at his memorial service

“Hi from the Unknown Soldier. I threw away my rifle and went swimming.

You may have seen me slipping away from the column. Shssssh.

If in a desert “theatre” I leave to go look at the night sky with all its stars—Aldeberan, Rigel, Spica, Eta Carinae.

I am a statue to the Noble Deserter in the park.”

I was inspired by artists like Tom Lewis! He had the “duende”—the spirit, the moxie. He had the will to continue in risky action after action of civil disobedience—from our blood pouring into the Plowshares movement.

Want to join us? Then **practice non-violence, resist war,** and don't forget to move to the left.

Forgive them, mother, for they know not what they do.

Heroes to follow? Tom Lewis, war resisters, Dan and Phil Berrigan,“Plowshares” activists, M. Gandhi, M.L. King, A.J. Muste, Dorothy Day, Quakers, Norman Morrison, Rachel Corrie, Brian Willson. . . .

2. “Once to Every Man and Nation”

Dave remakes the hymn: “Once to every man and nation.” Now politically correct—still moving: Dave's additions, transmogrifications in parens.

“Once to Every Man and Nation”: poem by James Russell Lowell (protesting America's war w Mexico—with apologies to James)—music tune nicknamed EBENEZER (one name like a Brazilian soccer star)—actually Ebenezer was arranged by Thomas John Williams, a Welsh organist. An Ebenezer is a stone of salvation after the stone monument erected by Samuel after a successful battle with the Philistines—it's in the Bible.

Stanza 1: “Once to every man (woman, trangendered person, animule, life form) comes the moment to decide.

In the strife of truth with falsehood (right wing, capitalist shit/crap) for the good or evil side.

Some great cause-God's (goddess, Buddha, Muhammed, Wiccan, abyss, nothing, quarks, muons,) God's new Messiah (Berrigan, King, (insert whomever for occasion), offering each the bloom or blight,

And (I love this part) the choice goes by forever 'twixt that darkness and that light.

Stanza 2: (Now picture this) By the light of burning martyrs, Jesus' bleeding feet I track. (can you believe the Unitarians have softened and changed the words in this hymn?)

Toiling up new Calvaries (movement/struggles, revolutions) ever with the cross that turns not back.

New occasions teach new duties (don't forget education), time makes ancient good uncouth (there's a stretch for a rhyme James),

They must onward still and onward, who would keep abreast of truth. (o yes)(still true!!!).

Stanza 3: Though the cause of evil (right wing stuff) prosper (how true), yet tis truth alone is strong (never forget it).

Though her portion be the scaffold, and upon the throne be wrong!!! (hmm—who's on the throne right about now?)

Yet that scaffold sways the future (think of John Brown at Charlestown) and behind the dim unknown (evolution, other planets more successful than ours?)

Standeth God (goddess, Buddha, Muhammed, Wiccan, abyss, nothing, quarks, muons,) within the shadow keeping watch above his/hers/its own (let's hope so) (you can see me read this on you tube)

3. Prophet Dave Remakes the "Sermon on the Mount" (Dave's in italics)

"Blessed are the meek, for they will inherit the earth." *Blessed are the meek for they shall not be right wing lawyers, politicians or capitalists. They shall be called protesters!! and let us forget not that militant non-violence can be VERRRY militant—not always turning the other cheek—bombing rail lines to Auschwitz, for example—or Weatherperson bombings of 70's (no one was hurt!).*

"Blessed are the merciful, for they will receive mercy." *Blessed are the kind—usually women—for they shall be a great relief and comfort to you who*

must stand in line at the bank or at the Dept. of Motor Vehicles or those who have to listen to or suffer at the hands of bombastic and violent men—(thank you Ntozake Shange).

"Blessed are the peacemakers, for they will be called children of God." *Blessed are the peacemakers for they shall offer all manner of civil disobedience and obstruction to the military and guns and the right wing! They shall throw sand in the gears of the military / industrial complex and shall enter military bases and offer symbolic protest. They shall offer real protest by destroying property that belongeth to the military! They shall be conscientious objectors and deserters and shall NOT obey orders—they shall be like Bradley Manning! i.e. wiki leaking. Eventually war shall be no more.*

"Blessed are those who are persecuted for righteousness' sake, for theirs is the kingdom of heaven." *Blessed are those who are persecuted for righteousness' sake for they shall usually be in courts like the supreme court in the U.S. that are run by the rich and the right wing... never forget that the golden rule is them that has the gold makes the rules, and the courts are structured accordingly. Never forget that capitalism maintains an underclass to lock up and fills its jails with them so that you will think something is being done about crime. The big criminals—politicians—those on wall street? they go scot free!*

Always worth remembering—**"Blessed are you when people revile you and persecute you and utter all kinds of evil against you falsely on my account. Rejoice and be glad, for your reward is great in heaven, for in the same way they persecuted the prophets who were before you."** ***And even if there is no heaven and there is no reward YOU ARE BLESSED!***

2 new "Blesseds":
Blessed are those who are absorbed and meditating, for that is one of the best places in the human condition to be in; they shall be placed in supreme paintings like Vermeer's!

Blessed are the children for they are absorbed in their play and the sounds they make are a benison to our ears and contrast mightily with the braying of politicians and people who are not on the left. e.g. after a big snow, children going down hills on inner tubes—or children at the public swimming pool!

Stations of the Cross

I held a cup of water as they dragged him by...
Troops wouldn't let you give him such a thing!

I felt it was momentous but knew not why...
The air that day just a bit heavier
(Which it usually isn't in desert countries);
Sarah's oleander bloomed white on her sill
The way it always does—the dates
At Micah's looked the same, some how
That day I felt sorry for the bum... felt my offering
As simple as it was, it meant something!—
Flash forward to Marcel Dupre's immense
Organ chords—"Stations of the Cross"—"He stumbles...
Jesus falls for the second time..."

They say we should set some aside for the poor...
They're almost festive, these parades, God knows—
Flash forward, Mantagnese's "10th Station"- Italian School—
Caravaggisti, I think it is—with heavy shadows?

"Jesus is stripped of his clothes."

One of his carpenter buddies offered
To help him carry- can you believe that?
The soldiers swatted him away- he was lucky, me
A cup of water, and he acknowledged, the sky
As blue as it gets—adamantine, actinic—

...and I've seen a thousand crucifixions.

Golgotha

from the repentant thief's perspective

At the moment of his dying he glances to his side...
That figure next to him, something about him...
What is he, gay or something? seems to know me?

The one in the middle? The pain comes in wave/flashes;
Like migraines, like white sand, blinding, Almagordo!
A sand storm would be nice! My vision blurring....

Blood fills my eyes, O death, please come!!
Thank God that soldier slipped me some kef*...
The one below to the side, I recognize him from the whore house.

Dear God, having never prayed before—forgive my sins, my lies,
What did the guy say—something about "paradise"?
My hearing's going! last chance to see the sun...

And after the first nail, it didn't get any goddamned easier,
That figure in the middle something about him!?!
Dear Lord I can stand the pain no more!!

We thieves thought we were slick—could beat the rap—
But this is no way to die? my setting sun!!
Blood fills my mouth—thank God for kat* to chew on!

My eyes glaze—what did he say about the "paradise"?
I swear I meant to change my life, at last, as if by magic
It's changed, I know it—was it me to change it?

Or him beside me? all growing very still.
The 3 of them shiver into death upon the hill.

My eyes are going now, my goddamned eyes.
But now I hear it clearly—*what he said!*
"Today thou shalt be with me in paradise."

* *Middle Eastern narcotics*

Another Biblical Poem

I am surrounded as if in ritual:
Smoke around me as if in ancient ritual?
Slow burn we do towards death—
We are not opposed to it, not totally—
Processional, approach the end with dignity—
And yet there's something there we do not like!

But the **word** for what it was escapes me for awhile
Only that I know it ends in an e
Sound, some kind of inspiration
And soft as myrrh, as autumn falls
Once more, wood smoke, sudden! coming to a
Long awaited conclusion and the **word**, finally,

is what?

Not sage or pine pungent—but
Sweet as myrrh, like must—tweeds in
A closet, when you open an old book...
Yet what's there seems dangerous
First wood fire after summer—
Odor of memory? Smell of death? The end has an e
Sound: as in "de profundis clamavi"?
"Out of the depths have I cried to thee".

How many springs must come and go, or summers?
What **word** is it specifically?
Light after a storm, say—in yellow fields,
And so we hope that things will be OK?
And yet we know they're things we simply cannot see!

That after storm feel—**epiphany**!

"Epiphany – 1. a Christian festival, observed on January 6, commemorating the Epiphany

2. manifestation of Christ to the gentiles in the persons of the Magi; Twelfth-day.

3. an appearance or manifestation, especially of a deity.

4. a sudden, intuitive perception of or insight into the reality or essential meaning of something, usually initiated by some simple, homely, or commonplace occurrence or experience.

5. a literary work or section of a work presenting, usually symbolically, such a moment of revelation and insight."

Homage to Hart Crane

His suicide's body plying currents in the Gulf stream...

O Hart you felt abandoned, unloved—you were wrong...

Like a Mayan maiden thrown into a cenote/well....

Your body sank like the Mayan pyramids rise

Over the scrub—the sacred roads—"sacbes"*...

Draped in sea whips, by orange sea sponges, the lace

Coral, watch dial radium green of sea shrimp signals**,

Along the reef wall, then down into the abyss...

Your body drifts—pale curtains of shark

In the distance—cordons of them in the cellophane sea...

O "laminate wrenches, o silver distentions";

Great rays shake sand off and flap into the horizon

As you pass—let us approach our muses as you did—as frankly

As we talk to ourselves—"nitroglycerin dunes, diazapam shoals"—

Even the date of your death (4.27.1932) has meaning....

And the Mayan calendar glyphs accorded you have great meaning....

* *pronounced: sock bays*
** *these found in Indonesia—the Banda Sea—not in the Caribbean*

Short Humorous Poems

1) Rampant Lizards

2) **Secret Rituals of the Bathroom Haiku** (some are by fellow PIB members)

tissue to be folded or bunched?
the flavor of
green tea over rice

the roiling bowl,
squirrels fighting
in the mulberry tree

what follows not by dme but fellow PIBsters (Poetry in Baltimore posters) (anyone want credit? Get in touch w me and I will add yr name–u deserve it—lol—yr work is pretty shitty by the way—dave)

"frog jumps in
my toilet—'plop'
top that Basho!

lock the bathroom door
I've got bizness to transact
some movements to conduct.

senator larry craig,
minneapolis airport....
footsies ensue

farting sounds sequenced
polite even numbers—
sounds like a plan

farewell faithful soldier
the waves of forgetfulness
call your name and bring you forth

how long i have waited
and i say goodbye
to my faithful children

trickle down slow and tired
i send my epistles
into nothingness

why is this delight

so quick and
memorable

once gone you are gone
forever
the finality of death and evacuation."

Short poem after Stephen Foster in a surrealist style and politically correct

"I'm coming, I'm coming
For my head is bending low.
I hear the bland arachnids calling
Old redneck Joe.

from Baltimore—home of the television series: "The Wire", "Homicide", "The Corner" (popular tv shows on crime in the ghetto)

1) Abandominium Ode

Rats b crawlin
cross my feet!
Heroin high!

2) Homage to David Mamet who did the original "Homicide" movie—set in B more in the 90's? 80's?

Serial killer to cop:
"Want to know the nature of evil?"
Cop: "No, I'd b out of a job!"

3) Homage to Mamet 2

"FBI couldn't find
Joe Louis
In a bowl of white rice!"

4)

Yo, careful that pit bull
Don't bite yr. johnson—
He b goin that way!

5) found poem

"Assistance for
Trapped animals?
Call 311"

Photo by Regina Walker

Homage to Harry Potter

You identify too much with frizzing whizzbees,
Me, I like orange berti botts.
Yr. whizzbees give me nothing but the willees!

Give em to muggles, now there's a thought,
Unless death eaters shake em silly,
Or inferis surround them with green snot.

I tried a cauldron cake, found it too gizzy,
And some one left my chocolate frogs to rot.
Draco Malfoy, now there's a skizzy,

But I'd trade him sickles if he had a knut.
Just leave me alone w yr. frizzing whizbees,
My friend is Merlin, yours—a monkey butt!

You sold yr. soul for frizzing whizzbees.
But ended w these frigging berti bots.

At the Large Hadron Collider near Geneva, Switzerland

Music the long searched for key to the door in the mountain and finding the door wasn't easy.

Going through the mountain not easy—warigs there—skittering bat like—you will smell them,

But once through past the last dragon—once through the mountain…

The professor with long hair gives you a tour of one of his parks—like a universe and

He demonstrates, tearing the edges of a vast curtain—it dissolves in a gyre.

"Watch the smell", he cautions, but it's nice—kind of buttery—"That's earth".

You are more grateful to music for having gotten you here—say how Chopin builds filigree

Upon filigree, or Shreker's "Chamber Symphony," keys keep dissolving….

You are certain the universe turns to some kind of music—you just can't hear it—but you are aware that it's there.

In some Grand Unified Theory, in the Large Hadron Collider near Geneva, they are searching!

A Visit to the Monocacy Battlefield, Frederick, Maryland

to Lieut. Geo. Davis and the 10th Regiment, Vt.

July 29, 2011

The engineers for the B & O Railroad had cleverly, non-violently solved the problem of crossing a canal over a river—where the lazy, Monocacy River passes into the Potomac near Point of Rocks—they constructed a bridge across the river that held water so that mules could haul the canal boats across! This bridge is still there—a fine jogging, bike path up from DC to Harper's Ferry—the C & O canal path.

Meanwhile upstream on the Monocacy in July of 1864, Confederates clashed with Federals at the battle of Monocacy—south of Frederick—2000 dead resulting! What was the mission? To take DC for the one, to defend the north from southern invasion for the other.

Was that enough to die for?

The Union soldiers had no way to know that before the Best Farm—smack in the middle of the battle, was once the L'Hermitage plantation where slaves were brutally treated—tortured even. And did the Federals feel they were fighting to free the slaves? Archaeology of the slave quarters is ongoing.

A young boy watched the battle unfold from behind a boarded up window at the Worthington farm—and today—in July the same river snakes through the field of battle to the Potomac—an unimpressive river—shallow—maybe a few good swimming holes—brown in color. The same shimmering heat obtains—the B & O trains plow regularly through as always on the way to Harpers Ferry. No river to die next to!! or was it? Is death in battle ever valid? Soldiers in Iraq and Afghanistan are today convinced that their sacrifice is warranted. At the moment of your death what would you be thinking?

Inconsolable sadness comes to me at the thought of a soldier's last day in this bucolic setting—were the grander battles at nearby Antietam and Gettysburg far more gallant fields on which to perish?—the florid lilt of 19th century expression does not help—as in "I have received my death wound—water. please give me water." I hate all wars, but still. . . .

To the boys Vermont, Pennsylvania, New Jersey* in these swales—

The bullets kicked up leaves, nicked branches—like hail-

stones in winter—"O Mattie—the boys and me took solace in the river, taking turns

(Altho the sound of musket/cannon burns. . .

A dull report—not sharp—too much like popping)...

We washed our stinking socks, I swear

There'd be some lovely farming here!

O Mattie although my love for country's grand—

I love you more—you and I could love this land!

If I should die here and you get this."

(But for cicadas, today all is still.)

"Please thank my tentmates—Owen, Will."

* *at the state monuments you are actually in Vt and NJ for they own the land—they pay considerably to maintain it.*

In the manner of the dialogue in the movie by the Coen brothers: "True Grit"—where all use a florid, old fashioned lingo

dedicated to fellow pib poet Mark Sanders (to b read with a sort of jolly menace in the manner of rooster cogburn—a character in the book and movie)

we tuk the sanders boy

...from over at the "spk yore peece" saloon?

we bushed him down by the sedge

over on the julie fisher spread...

we wuz fixin to hang im cuz he was so purty—

he wasn't like the rest of us ar kansians

but we was just a funnin w him and we told him

to speek purty for us, ? says he's a poetry boy?

snow started fallin on cedars at abt that time,

down by the missouri breaks—we wuz a fordin the river

me and the gurl—lil emily d we call her—

i'm playin w sanders—showed him the rope awrite

then my sharps rifle? that got his attention—

but he red reel good and we let im go this time

At the Tomb of Poe, a Sonnet

He sinks beneath the surface like a stone,
Sidling crab wise down 'til buried in mud,
A gold bug thread wise through vacant skull eye down
Into maelstroms of stars. Less and less loud, the thud,
Of shovelfuls above him.... into sidereal time, the tunnel back to light
obscured....
Buried alive as he thought! As if to keep him down, the green
Block from some ancient, obscure disaster—Vermont granite dug,
Ripton quarried, dark green, not jadeite green, an intenser, darker green—
As absinthe, but blacker, still, like "Nevermore", its dense sheen
Like shiny hair: black hair, Ligea's, Virginia's, Helen's or Lenore's.
Bury the critics alive, I say, Poe careens
Down corridors of light, more drunk than before!!

Upon the stone a raven carved, the words blur, but it's not the end.
Buried alive in our imaginations, he rises eerily, again!

Dave and Medea Benjamin of Code Pink before Bradley Manning demo

Brechtian Political Poem

to Diane DiPrima

if Che stood before you giving a speech?
u'd probably b rubbing your eyes?

che recited león felipe's poem*
to sugar cane workers

and one wonders what they thought?
the poem somewhat surreal...

from the coca leaf
to street cocaine... what percentage?

Under socialsm the drugs
Will not b "stepped on"...

capitalism... hello marketing...
top fortunes listed,

some of them "shipping",
as to off shore islands, swiss banks...

and yet the desperate
must make a living—whichever, whataway...

paris commune ('71) banned prostitution...
why should female body b considered a commodity?

or the woman b forced to
consider herself so?

do you see what
we're up against?

in that the profit
from what is desired

becomes exploitable?

Medea and Code Pink members at Bradley Manning demo—Quantico, Virginia

and workers may not b paid?!?!?

murder becomes a
"resolution of conflict"

under the "marketing dept.",
o we all need a buzz

so why not legalize buzzes? distribute wealth
to the mules!

mexican drug wars
pit workers v workers. . .

and in u.s.—fannie mae, freddy mac, standard poor,
was not the bankers either

paid a price
but workers do!

until a government puts
people before profits

do you want to b played like
a monkey in a cage?

the mexican police?
are you glad you're under

rule of "law" in u.s.?
check disparity between

crack and
powder cocaine. . .

follow the money. . .
see where it gets you. . .

** the Felipe poem that Che read? "The rose of flour"—also in Che's Green Notebook: surely one of the greatest poems in the Spanish language*

Police at Quantico arrested 30—they did not yield.

Mark Sanders poster

Alex Fine poster

About the Author

David Eberhardt was born in March, 1941. As a peace protester, he was incarcerated at Lewisburg Federal Prison for pouring blood on draft files in 1967 with Father Phil Berrigan and two others to protest the Vietnam war. He retired from work in the criminal IN justice system in 2010 after 33 years of work at the Baltimore City Jail (see Chapter "Offender Aid and Restoration—on the website".) Two previous books of poetry are available: *The Tree Calendar* (Dolphin Moon Press, 1987) and *Blue Running Lights* (Abecedarian Press, 2007). More of Dave's work can be found at http://davideberhardt.webs.com/.

www.ingramcontent.com/pod-product-compliance
Lightning Source LLC
LaVergne TN
LVHW052258100826
845147LV00001B/86

* 9 7 8 0 9 8 2 1 8 5 4 2 1 *